reflections

A CALLIGRAPHIC JOURNEY
THROUGH THE
WISDOM OF WORDS

JIM BILLINGSLEY

ISBN: 1 86476 016 8

TO JADE

CHRISTMAS 2022

LOVE FROM

AUNTY FIONA XO

Here is a collection of words.

Words that may uplift you.

Just as a melody will lock in
your memory - so can words.

Be in no hurry to read them.

Open this book at any page.

CALLIGRAPHY & ILLUSTRATIONS
BY JIM BILLINGSLEY

IF YOU CAN KEEP YOUR HEAD
WHEN ALL ABOUT YOU
ARE LOSING THEIRS AND
BLAMING IT ON YOU;
IF YOU CAN TRUST YOURSELF
WHEN ALL MEN DOUBT YOU,
BUT MAKE ALLOWANCE FOR
THEIR DOUBTING TOO;

IF YOU CAN WAIT AND NOT
BE TIRED BY WAITING,
OR, BEING LIED ABOUT,
DON'T DEAL IN LIES,
OR BEING HATED
DON'T GIVE WAY TO HATING,
AND YET DON'T LOOK TOO GOOD,
NOR TALK TOO WISE;
IF YOU CAN DREAM ~ AND
NOT MAKE DREAMS YOUR
MASTER;

IF YOU CAN THINK ~ AND
NOT MAKE THOUGHTS YOUR
AIM,
IF YOU CAN MEET WITH
TRIUMPH AND DISASTER
AND TREAT THOSE TWO
IMPOSTERS JUST THE SAME:
IF YOU CAN BEAR TO HEAR
THE TRUTH YOU'VE SPOKEN
TWISTED BY KNAVES TO MAKE
A TRAP FOR FOOLS, OR
WATCH THE THINGS YOU
GAVE YOUR LIFE TO, BROKEN,

AND STOOP AND BUILD 'EM
UP WITH WORN-OUT TOOLS;
IF YOU CAN MAKE ONE HEAP
OF ALL YOUR WINNINGS
AND RISK IT ON ONE TURN
OF PITCH-AND-TOSS, AND
LOSE, AND START AGAIN AT
YOUR BEGINNINGS, AND
NEVER BREATHE A WORD
ABOUT YOUR LOSS:
IF YOU CAN FORCE YOUR
HEART AND NERVE AND

SINEW TO SERVE YOUR TURN
LONG AFTER THEY ARE GONE,'
AND SO HOLD ON WHEN THERE IS
NOTHING IN YOU EXCEPT
THE WILL WHICH SAYS TO THEM :
'HOLD ON'!
IF YOU CAN TALK WITH
CROWDS AND KEEP YOUR
VIRTUE, OR WALK WITH
KINGS ~ NOR LOSE THE
COMMON TOUCH,
IF NEITHER FOES NOR LOVING

FRIENDS CAN HURT YOU,
IF ALL MEN COUNT WITH YOU,
BUT NONE TOO MUCH:
IF YOU CAN FILL THE
UNFORGIVING MINUTE
WITH SIXTY SECONDS' WORTH
OF DISTANCE RUN, YOURS
IS THE EARTH AND
EVERYTHING THAT'S IN IT,
AND-WHICH IS MORE —
YOU'LL BE A MAN,
MY SON!

Rudyard Kipling

The sky
a tree &
and man
will survive
if man
understands
the tree

mm billingsley

THE CLOUDS SKIP ACROSS THE SKY
THEY DON'T KNOW
WHAT LIFE IS GOING ON DOWN HERE
NOR DO THEY CARE

THEY ARE COLLECTIONS OF TEARS
AND WHEN THEY CRY
THE WORLD BLOOMS BECAUSE
IT IS THE BEGINNING OF LIFE

WHEN I CRY
~NOTHING HAPPENS.

Kathryn MacKenzie-Smith

Gentleness

Hold that bubble gently child
~See the shimmer of rainbow light
Savour the moment look in wonder~
At the depth of gentleness.

Set that bubble to the air~
See the colours everywhere
A floating sphere of spectrum light
To each child a sheer delight.

A bubble is a gossamer wing
Born aloft by zephyr wind
Akin the condor bird in flight
His shadow is never above his sight.

Peter Brooks   Poem for Year of the Child

When you see the world
as part of yourself,
You will take care of it.

When you see yourself
as part of the world,

You will be taken care of.

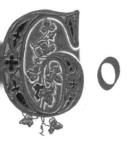
O

placidly amid the noise and haste, and remember what peace there may be in silence. As far as possible without surrender be on good terms with all persons. Speak your truth quietly and clearly; and listen to others, even the dull and ignorant, they too have their story. Avoid loud and aggressive persons, they are vexations to the spirit. If you compare yourself with others, you may become vain and bitter; for always there will be greater and lesser persons than yourself. Enjoy your achievements as

WELL AS YOUR PLANS. KEEP INTERESTED IN YOUR OWN CAREER, HOWEVER HUMBLE; IT IS A REAL POSSESSION IN THE CHANGING FORTUNES OF TIME. EXERCISE CAUTION IN YOUR BUSINESS AFFAIRS; FOR THE WORLD IS FULL OF TRICKERY. BUT LET NOT THIS BLIND YOU TO WHAT VIRTUE THERE IS; MANY PERSONS STRIVE FOR HIGH IDEALS; AND EVERYWHERE LIFE IS FULL OF HEROISM. BE YOURSELF. ESPECIALLY, DO NOT FEIGN AFFECTION. NEITHER BE CYNICAL ABOUT LOVE; FOR IN THE FACE OF ALL ARIDITY AND DISENCHANTMENT IT IS AS PERENNIAL AS THE GRASS. TAKE KINDLY THE COUNCIL OF THE YEARS, GRACEFULLY SURRENDERING THE THINGS OF YOUTH. NURTURE STRENGTH OF SPIRIT TO SHIELD YOU IN SUDDEN MISFORTUNE. BUT DO NOT DISTRESS yourself with imaginings. Many fears are born of fatigue and loneliness. Beyond a wholesome discipline, be gentle with yourself. You are a child of the universe, no less than the trees and the stars; you have a right to be here. And whether or not it is clear to you, no doubt the universe is unfolding as it should. Therefore be at peace with God, whatever you conceive Him to be. And whatever your labours and aspirations, in the noisy confusion of life keep peace with your soul. With all its sham, drudgery and broken dreams, it is still a beautiful world. Be cheerful, strive to be happy.

If wrinkles must be written upon our brows, let them not be written upon the heart. The spirit should not grow old.

James A. Garfield

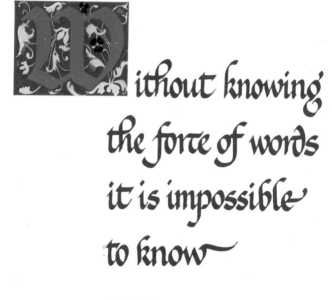

ithout knowing
the force of words
it is impossible
to know
man.

MONEY

Buys everything
except love,
personality,
freedom,
and
immortality.

ALL IS WELL

DEATH IS NOTHING AT ALL
I HAVE ONLY SLIPPED INTO THE NEXT ROOM
I AM I AND YOU ARE YOU
WHATEVER WE WERE TO EACH OTHER
THAT WE STILL ARE

CALL ME BY MY OLD FAMILIAR NAME
SPEAK TO ME IN THE EASY WAY WHICH
YOU ALWAYS USED
PUT NO DIFFERENCE
IN YOUR TONE

WEAR NO FORCED AIR OF SOLEMNITY
OR SORROW
LAUGH AS WE ALWAYS LAUGHED AT THE
LITTLE JOKES WE ENJOYED TOGETHER
PLAY, SMILE, THINK OF ME, PRAY FOR ME
LET MY NAME BE EVER THE HOUSEHOLD
WORD THAT IT EVER WAS

LET IT BE SPOKEN WITHOUT EFFECT
WITHOUT THE TRACE OF A SHADOW ON IT
LIFE MEANS ALL THAT IT EVER MEANT
IT IS THE SAME AS IT EVER WAS
THERE IS ABSOLUTELY UNBROKEN
CONTINUITY
WHY SHOULD I BE OUT OF MIND
BECAUSE I AM OUT OF SIGHT?
I AM BUT WAITING FOR YOU
~FOR AN INTERVAL
SOMEWHERE VERY NEAR
JUST AROUND THE CORNER

The Tree

YOU WHO WOULD PASS BY
AND RAISE YOUR HAND AGAINST ME
~ LISTEN BEFORE YOU HARM ME
I AM THE HEAT OF YOUR HEARTH
ON LONG WINTER NIGHTS,
THE FRIENDLY SHADE SCREENING YOU
FROM THE SUMMER SUN,
AND MY FRUITS ARE REFRESHING DRAUGHTS.

I AM THE BEAM THAT HOLDS YOUR HOUSE,
THE BOARD OF YOUR TABLE,
THE BED ON WHICH YOU LIE,
AND THE TIMBER WHICH BUILDS YOUR BOAT.

PRAYER

I AM THE HANDLE OF YOUR HOE,
AND THE DOOR OF YOUR HOMESTEAD,

I AM THE WOOD OF YOUR CRADLE,
AND THE SHELL OF YOUR COFFIN.

I AM THE GIFT OF GOD & FRIEND OF MAN.
YOU WHO PASS BY ME
LISTEN TO MY PRAYER
AND HARM ME NOT.

The most difficult
thing in life
is to
know yourself.

Thales

If Today~

If you planted hope today
In any hopeless heart,
If someone's burden was lighter
Because you did your part,
If you caused a laugh
That chased some tears away
If tonight your name is named
When someone kneels to pray
Then-your day
Has been well spent.

EASY

TO GET DEPRESSED THESE DAYS,
EASY TO FEEL AFRAID,
EASY TO THINK THE WORLD'S GONE MAD,
EASY FOR DREAMS TO FADE.
BUT THE NEWS WE HEAR OF THINGS WE FEAR
SHOULD NEVER BLIND US TO
THE MANY KIND AND SPLENDID THINGS,
SO MANY PEOPLE DO.

JUST ABOUT ANY DREAM GROWS STRONGER IF YOU HOLD ON A LITTLE LONGER.

Margo Gina Hart

TIS THE LAST ROSE OF SUMMER
   LEFT BLOOMING ALONE;
      ALL HER LOVELY COMPANIONS
      ARE FADED AND GONE;
         NO FLOWER OF HER KINDRED,
         NO ROSE BUD IS NIGH,
            TO REFLECT BACK HER BLUSHES,
            OR GIVE HER SIGH FOR SIGH.

I'LL NOT LEAVE THEE, THOU LONE ONE!
   TO PINE ON THE STEM;
      SINCE THE LOVELY ARE SLEEPING,
      GO TO SLEEP THOU WITH THEM.
         THUS KINDLY I SCATTER
         THY LEAVES O'ER THE BED,
            WHERE THY MATES OF THE GARDEN
            LIE SCENTLESS AND DEAD.

SO SOON MAY I FOLLOW,
   WHEN FRIENDSHIPS DECAY,
      AND FROM LOVE'S SHINING CIRCLE
      THE GEMS DROP AWAY.
         WHEN TRUE HEARTS LAY WITHER'D
         AND FOND ONES ARE FLOWN,
            OH, WHO WOULD INHABIT
            THIS BLEAK WORLD ALONE?

happiness is as a butterfly,
which, when pursued, is always
just beyond our grasp,
but which,
if you will sit down quietly,
may alight upon you.

Nathaniel Hawthorne

Middle·age is when you know
your·way ·round, but don't
feel · like·going.

In giving and receiving
we learn to love and be loved;
we encounter the meaning of life,
the mystery of existence.

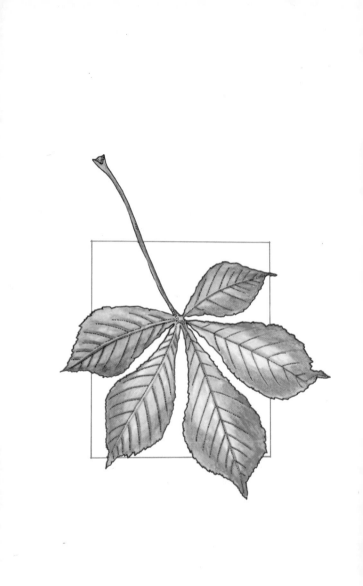

One night I had a dream…
I dreamed I was walking along the beach
with God and across the sky flashed
scenes from my life. For each scene I
noticed two sets of footprints in the sand,
one belonged to me and the other to God.

When the last scene of my life flashed
before us I looked back at the footprints
in the sand.

I noticed that at times along the path
of life there was only one set of
footprints.

I also noticed that it happened at the
very lowest and saddest times of my life.

This really bothered me and I questioned
God about it.

'God, you said that once I decided to follow you, you would walk with me all the way, but I noticed that during the most troublesome time in my life there is only one set of footprints.

I don't understand why in times I needed you most, you would leave me.' God replied, 'My precious, precious child, I love you and I would never, never leave you during your times of trials and suffering.

When you see only one set of footprints it was then that I carried you'...

'I expect to pass through this world but once, therefore any good that I can do or any kindness that I can show to any fellow creature, let me do it now; let me not defer it or neglect it, for I shall not pass this way again.'

Stephen Grellett 1773~1855

Music is the poetry
of sound.

Jim Billingsley

When some great sorrow,
like a mighty river,
Flows through your life
with peace-destroying power,
And dearest things are
swept from sight forever,
Say to your heart
each trying hour:
'This, too, shall pass away.'

Lanta Wilson Smith

PERHAPS THE STRAIGHT

AND NARROW PATH

WOULD BE WIDER

IF MORE PEOPLE

USED IT.

KAY INGRAM

sharing

We share our happiness with each other—
and it becomes greater.

We share our troubles with each other
and they become smaller.

We share one another's griefs & burdens—
and their weight becomes possible to bear.

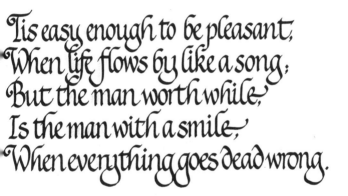

'Tis easy enough to be pleasant,
When life flows by like a song;
But the man worth while,
Is the man with a smile,
When everything goes dead wrong.

Ella Wheeler Wilcox

AY THE ROAD R
MAY THE WIND B
MAY THE SUN SHII
THE RAIN FALL SOF
AND, UNTIL WE M
MAY GOD HOLD YO

ıp to meet you,
ɔays at your back
rm upon your face
ɔn your fields
again,
the palm of his hand.

There is a wonderful, mystical law of nature that the three things we crave most in life - happiness, freedom, and peace of mind - are always attained by giving them to someone else.

DO ALL THE GOOD YOU CAN,
BY ALL THE MEANS YOU CAN,
IN ALL THE WAYS YOU CAN,
IN ALL THE PLACES YOU CAN,
AT ALL THE TIMES YOU CAN,
TO ALL THE PEOPLE YOU CAN,

AS LONG AS EVER YOU CAN.

John Wesley

Age is what the onlooker sees — not what the looked.upon feels.

Be glad for work that's difficult,
For tasks that challenge you!
Workers find a thousand blessings
The idle never knew.

ACKNOWLEDGEMENTS TO
KATHRYN MacKENZIE-SMITH
& PETER BROOKS FOR THEIR
CONTRIBUTION TO THIS
COLLECTION.

JB